THE SECRETS

BEHIND

CLOSED

DOORS

Wounded For Purpose

ALISA D. WIMBLEY

Love Clones Publishing
www.lcpublishing.net

Printed in the United States of America

First Printing, 2016

ISBN: 978-1519164803

Scripture quotations marked "KJV" are taken from the Holy Bible, King James Version (Public Domain)

Publishers:
Love Clones Publishing
Dallas, TX 75205
www.lcpublishing.net

DEDICATION

I want to first give honor to God for who He is in my life. I'm so thankful and grateful for Him guiding my path and watching over me daily, keeping me safe and sound. I thank Him for not allowing the enemy to destroy me as I was going through my process. I praise God because His hand is on my life. I'm thankful for how He changed my entire life around and positioned me back on the right path. No matter what I've done or where I have been, God loves me.

So today I submit and surrender my life and my written book into His hands, praying that He will bless it and allow my life journey to help other women who have been sexually and physical abused. I'm writing to let them know that there's a way out behind the closed doors. God has already prepared an open door just for you.

ACKNOWLEGEMENTS

I want to honor and thank my parents Dave and Fannie Howard for releasing me to write about my early childhood years. Thanking God for the valuable relationship that I have with both of my parents today; praising God for the coming together that has taken place in our life today. God has truly joined us closer together, and has healed our hearts and life greatly. I honor and thank God for it all.

I want to acknowledge and honor my children my oldest son Louis, his wife Shanea and baby Nathan and my baby boy Kevin.

Next, I want to next honor my siblings who I love dearly. Dave Howard Jr., my only brother who's the apple of my eye. I want to honor and thank all of my sisters that God has blessed me with, Tebrena Fears, Shirene Hicks, Kierra Howard, Stepanie Streeter Edwards, Keatha Keys. I love them so much; they're so special to me.

I give honor to my Spiritual Father/Pastor, Apostle Jonathan L. Swain who has labored with me for years, assisting me in getting delivered from my childhood pass issues and hurts. I want to salute him and thank him for his time, and years he invested in my life. I will never forget him.

I want to honor my Spiritual mother, Prophetess Kathy Hemphill for her labor of love towards me. I want to thank her for all the correction and that helped pushed me into purpose, building me up when I was weak, and pushing me to stay on the right path. I love and appreciate your labor of love towards me.

I want to honor my best friends Shaletha Malden, who lead me back to the feet of Jesus. I thank God for eighteen years of friendship. Also, Alice Williams, Kanitha Johnson Crangle, and Gwendolyn Cannon for years of friendship. These women have been by my side for years. I want to take a moment to honor my Godly friendships and those who have invested into my life.

I want to thank and honor Pastor Karen Jackson, for her encouragement all the way through my writing process. She pushed me from the beginning to the end of my assignment to complete and finish the process. Thanking and praising God, for putting you in my life to help birth out my book.

FOREWORD

The "Secrets Behind Close Doors" is a strong read on the facts of life. It is a truth on the reality of what shapes and makes us in the early stages of our lives. This book will take you on an emotional roller coaster that in the end will cause you to see your life and also to see the hand of God in it.

The Secrets Behind Close Door tells the story of old school generational thought process that what goes on in the house stays in the house. Here the writer knows that in order for her to move forward and be whom God has called for her, she most come from behind the closed door. The writer's intent in this read is to tell test and trails, not to bring shame and embarrassment to any one, but to bring the real deliverance to the people of God. Sometimes we are not free because we continue to live in the past. Therefore the writer believes to have real freedom you must deal with the real issues of life and confront them. When we deal with our issues. Then we can be delivered from those things we have had to deal with in life.

The writings in this book will cause the reader to desire to be their true self and be delivered from anything in the past and or current life that would stop them from getting to their place as to where God has called them. Secrets Behind Close Doors is about helping people and those connected to those who are hurt and or broken. This story will even heal those that knew what happened to others in life and didn't know how and or what to do. Reading this book itself will bring on a level or measure of deliverance. This book is raw and real but it is also reading for it makes us face our own realities and be thanks for where we are in life today and with God.

This book is a must read and you will need to share it with your family and friend so that deliverance can take place on a large scale. My hats goes off to the writer for telling a story that even in her pain, it will bring people to a place of seeking and trusting God for a greater place of freedom. Knowing that my past might have helped shape my present and will not dictate my promise in God.

Apostle Jonathan L. Swain
Senior Pastor
God's True Love Outreach Ministries
1618 W 65th Street "Church"
Send mailings to 6455 S Marshfield Ave
Chicago, Illinois 60636-2715
773-922-8160 - Ministry Phone
www.GTLOM.org - Website

FOREWORD

Alisa Wimbley, is an amazing of women of God. I count it as an honor to have her as a spiritual daughter. Alisa is a gifted and humble servant. She uses her gifts both naturally and spiritually; she is a nurse, an ordained Evangelist, with a Masters in Divinity and her labor is for the building of God's kingdom. Her heart of love and compassion is for God's people, especially broken women.

We are all traveling on this road call life. Many have endured sadness and hardship on their journey through life. Some may even wonder, am I along on this journey or can I survive this pain. Alisa's willingness to open up and share her story about the Secrets Behind Close Doors will help many to understand the importance of not giving up. Knowing that God's purpose for your life is not based on how you are treated or what people think of you. I believe reading Alisa Wimbley's book, The Secrets Behind Close Doors will help others to let go of their past hurt, their shame and un-forgiveness. The Secrets Behind Close Doors is a spiritual eye opener. As you begin to read this book you will see how Alisa's tragedies became stepping-stones to her destiny.

Lady Kathy Hemphill
Co-Pastor
New Assembly of Holiness Church
Chicago, IL

CHAPTER 1

IS IT TRAGEDY OR DESTINY?

I didn't consider my early years of life to be normal. I was born to teenage parents who met in High School and quickly fell in love. Back in the sixty's it wasn't abnormal for people to fall in love at such a young age, or get married early is life. I believe love was truly in the air for both of them. They became inseparable and very attached to each other, at least that's what I was told. Their love and bond was so strong they felt this was the kind of relationship that would last a lifetime, although my mom was only sixteen, and my father was a young inexperienced seventeen years old. Yet, they knew their love for each other was real and true. Their strong love quickly turned into a desire and passion for each other that neither one of them could refrain from the desire to be intimate. After they gave into this desire my mother became pregnant and gave birth to me. I was their first-born child together. Born in my grandparent's home with the assistance of a midwife. Yes, back then babies were born at home. Their endearment and deep affection for each other didn't stop with just my birth. Exactly three years later my mom gave birth to my brother. This took place before they were joined together in marriage. Shortly after giving birth to my little brother my parents finally tied the knot!

Maybe they didn't realize their decision to get married would come with a greater price tag then dating. However, we still continued to live with my grandparents because my parents weren't financially stable. My parents' decision to get married started with a family they'd already started. This forced them into adulthood quickly, causing them to make some life changing decisions for our family. My father wasn't financially prepared for this level of life, but he was excited about our new beginning. He moved to Chicago, leaving us behind for a while, determined to provide for his family. His goal was to work, be productive and successful. In 1973, after six months of working and saving up money, my father returned to Mississippi to get us. As I reflect back, I can remember the ride to Chicago, it seemed like I cried all the way there. Although the plan was always for us to move together as a family, I was not happy or excited about the move. I was only four years old at the time, and I did not want to leave my Nanna. I bonded well with my Nanna, I didn't want to depart from her and live with a man I hardly knew. You may be wondering how can she say I hardly knew him when he was only gone for six months. Well, in my four-year old mind, my mom, my brother and I didn't need a home because I loved being in my Nanna and grandpa's home. Although my dad would come and visit us I did not really spend much time with him. For one, he had a hairy face and I "feared the beard!" I remember when he would come to see me; I would run and hide in my Nanna's room. I can recall my Nanna calling me out of her bedroom to spend time with my father. So yes, I hardly knew him because at the time we weren't living under the same roof.

Looking back, I can remember that I cried and cried on the way to Chicago. I cried so much until it landed me my first *whooping*. My father pulled the car over and let me have it. I was kicking, yelling and screaming. Truly, this would be an adjustment for me. I was thinking, why did my mom allow this stranger to take us away from our home. Was this move a tragedy or my destiny?

After arriving in the windy city we moved into our own apartment for a few years. My father's aunt helped him purchased his first apartment in the same building she lived in. My parents were blessed with a new home on the west side of Chicago a few years later. My father's dad assisted my parents in purchasing their first home. My parents were happy and very content. My father couldn't keep his hands off of my mother, their passion for each other grew so strong over the years. I could remember as a child, that my house was getting bigger and larger with more siblings. It seemed like my mom was pregnant often. Our family grew quickly; I soon had a lot of sisters and one brother living with me. I lived with my six siblings in a two-bedroom home.

Well, it eventually became seven of us because by father had two other daughters before he married my mom. And one daughter came to live with us when she was twelve years old. This house was jammed packed with people. This was the home that I lived in until I grew up and married.

Before I formed thee in the belly I knew thee and before thou camest forth out of the wound I sanctified thee, and I ordained thee a prophet unto the nations. -Jeremiah 1:5

CHAPTER 2

STRICT AND RESTRICTED

My parents began attending Church services with my great aunt. The church was called Faith Church of God in Christ on the west side of Chicago. My parents decided to give their life to the Lord at that time, and began raising my siblings and I in holiness. It appeared to be strange to me. We had to attend church all of our childhood years. We grew up in a church with strict holiness teaching. Most of the teaching I did not quite understand as a child. We were in church three to four times a week. It seemed like all day and all night to me. My parents' spiritual beliefs were very different from my peers. Church was their entire life. The teaching was so firm and uncompromising and difficult to follow as a child. I don't truly understand why but I wasn't allowed to do normal everyday things. Back then it appeared to me that everything was considered a sinful behavior or desire.

They spent a huge amount of time in church serving and donating their time to the work of the ministry. I could remember my parents' faithfulness to the Lord's house was great. They would never miss a service.

My parents didn't allow us to participate in much of anything growing up. Playing sports, going to see a movie, attend parties, or participating in after school activities were definitely a *NO.*" My parents believed that many of these activities were sins and very unproductive. I know now that your relationship with God has to do with your love and pure heart before him. Repentance is the key; wearing long dresses to your ankle had nothing to do with a true lifestyle before God. The way you dress play sports or participate in school activities doesn't affect your personal walk with God.

Longing just to be normal, and to participate in regular childhood activities was my heart desire as a child. Sometimes on the weekend, my parents would allow us to play ball at the basketball court down the street.

I remember my Father would say, "If any man comes to the basketball court leave and come home!" Well that was mostly all the time that a man would come to the basketball court. I remember times when I wouldn't leave when someone else came to the court and my Dad would find out and I would get slapped in my face for not obeying. That slapping a lot of the time would take place outside in the open where all the kids and neighbors on the block would see. I was a very hard-headed and disobedient child growing up. I just wanted to do more as a child, but was restricted and on lock down daily. Growing up was like living in a prison.

Being raised in a Christian home made us so different from other people. I was different from my classmates. I did not dress like them at all. I stood out like a sore thumb every day in my skirts or dresses. They were wearing pants, and here I was wearing my skirts daily, even in the freezing cold. It was not like I wanted to wear skirts, but in our house it was mandatory. I grew up thinking that everyone who wore skirts and dresses were the only people going to heaven. That Jesus would only be coming back for them. I didn't know any better at that time. And no, I did not want to be different, I wanted to fit in and be a part of the "IN" crowd, but I was not. I was strange and peculiar to most, even to myself. My childhood was brought under strict and firm teaching; teachings that I had to adhere to at home and at church. My childhood was like a whirlwind, blowing continually. I remember thinking that this isn't the way life should be. I don't want to live like this; I just wanted to fit in. I didn't like being different. I spent a great deal of my life trying to be a part but because I didn't fit in, I felt rejected. This is where the spirit of rejection entered in. Very early in life, I was challenged with this spirit.

But ye {are} a chosen generation, a royal priesthood, a holy nation, a peculiar people, that ye should shew forth the praises of him who called you out of darkness into his marvelous light. -1 Peter 2:9

CHAPTER 3

SUNGLASSES ON A RAINY DAY

My childhood was very strange and disturbing to me. Even though, Church was my family life and I grew up under very strict and hard religious teaching, there was another side behind the scene that wasn't revealed to others. We churched three to four days a week, my parents loved

God and they served in the Church faithful. There life was dedicated to the things of God, but underneath we had a deep dark side that wasn't open to the public. There were many issues and secrets behind closed doors. All were masked by the outer appearance, but the inside was private

and silent. Covered beneath a place of darkness.

I grew up very close to my mom. Well, all of my siblings were close to mom. She was a very caring and loving parent to all of us, always treating us equally. She loved us unconditionally. Now on the other hand, I didn't feel quite the same type of love from my father. My dad was very verbal about his chosen child. The entire household knew and understood that my baby sister at that time was his favored. The writing was on the wall.

I could recall many days my dad would come after me for something. I felt like a target to him. I would look for mom to get him off of me. On many occasions mom had to jumped between my dad and I. She would attempt to protect and defend me most of the time, but he would just push her out of the way. Sometimes he would continually beat me until I was lifeless. Usually he would stop when I stopped moving, stiff and laying there because I had no more fight in me. Many years my father would literally fight me like I was a man. I remember always thinking and wondering as a child, what did I do to deserve being treated like this. "What was wrong with me". "Why didn't he love me?"

My father was physically, emotionally and mentally abusive. As a child I was so afraid of my father. I was silent and broken inside unable to speak or articulate my opinions and feelings. I would keep everything bundled up inside, I had no voice. I was truly afraid of sharing my true feelings with my parents.

I remember my father's favorite sentence he would say to me often was, "you will never be nothing in life; you will never accomplish anything in life." I can remember those words so strong in me. It was on repeat for years.

I heard, "you will never be anything, you're a failure". Anything your hands touch will fail. I would hear these words when I was awake and when I was sleep. They were attached to me like a magnet.

I began to think that there was no reason in attempting and trying to achieve anything, since I was already a failure. If I wasn't going to be successful at anything in life, then why even try.

Growing up I wasn't able to express myself. Most of the time I just cried myself to sleep. My father's words were law, and nothing else was said after that. I remember like it was yesterday, when dad would come home from work you could hear a pen fall on the carpet.

We were too afraid to make a sound or to move around too much while he was home, we didn't want to draw any attention to ourselves.

My father appeared very angry and evil to me, not really understanding as a child why he was so mad all the time. It appeared to me, that I was his personal punching bag. I grew up so fearful and scared of my dad. The spirit of fear overtook me; it gripped my heart bad. I'm not the only sibling with a story to tell, my brother and sisters were frightened as well at that time.

After a bad day at work, my father would come home upset ready to release whatever built up anger that was a result of that day. He wanted the house quiet, which was impossible with the amount of people living in a two bedroom house. Peacefulness was not inside our house, too many people lived there.

My father had a lot of rules we had to learn to follow. My father taught us early how to communicate and respond back to them as our parents.

We were taught to reply yes sir/ma'am, and no sir/ma'am. He demanded that respect daily. This was how we communicated with them daily and if you made a mistake, and forgot he would go upside our heads with his fist.

On many occasions I would forget to address my parents before speaking with them. This act would leave me being punished or with bruises. My father believed in corporate punishment, meaning belts, brooms, extension cords, switches whatever he could grab first to correct me. I was beaten multiple times wearing just my underwear and T-shirt, I recall attending school many days with a black or red shot eye half way close.

I can recall a particular situation, that landed me one of my black eyes. One night, after my dad came home from work, he was sitting in the dining room watching television and relaxing. He called me from the bedroom to bring him a cold glass of water. Well, I had just finished washing the dishes and I grabbed a glass without rinsing it out. I filled the glass up with water, and handed it to my dad. I didn't realize there was dish washing liquid still sitting in the bottom of the glass.

So I served my father, a large cup of soapy water, which landed me another black eye, and a slap in my face with his fist. My father jumped up so fast out of his sit, I don't know what was wrong. I wasn't really paying attention to what I was doing. He scared my so bad, my heart almost jumped out of my chest. Frighten out of my skin, and I almost urinated myself. Well that was a reminder to pay more attention to the glasses I would serve him.

Going to school with sunglasses on my face and whelps all over my arms and legs, was beginning to cause attention. While attending elementary school people began to ask me questions about my household. Questions like, why are you wearing sunglasses in the class room? Which most of the time I was lying and defending my home. My teacher would yell out, take those sun glasses off in my classroom. You're not allowed to wear them. Once I recall answering many questions from my peers concerning my black and blue eyes. Continually lying and making up false information to try and cover up the real story. My best response was I got into another fight with kids in my neighborhood. Not wanting to reveal to people what was really going on behind closed doors. I was so afraid of probably suffering the consequences after sharing too much personal information at school.

I could remember one Wednesday morning after arriving at school, after I took off my jacket, my teacher began questioning me about the whelps and red marks on my arms. Sitting in the front of the classroom, her eyes was always on me.

Before I knew it my teacher had called the principal to the classroom. I was questioned in depth by instructors and workers. Within an hour, I was called to the office on the main floor. As I walked into the office, I noticed the people in the office wearing big badges on their jackets. They introduced themselves as the Department of Family Services.

Two of the ladies called me behind the office desk, and took me in a back room. And as I followed them into the room they asked me, if I would show them my arms and back, and legs. As they we're putting on their gloves to begin to assess me, they explained to me, that they were looking for marks and bruises that were put on me.

As they were looking over my body, the lady began asking me a ton of questions. Being so afraid of the outcome of their body check. I began to beg and plead with the people with the badges, telling them that I was okay. Nothing was wrong with me, I just have a lot of fights in my neighborhood. Knowing in my heart and mind that this was not the truth. I got along great with all the kids on my block, but I truly didn't want my father to be exposed. I was extremely fearful of my dad's reaction.

As I was attempting to explain to them, they were still questioning me. Asking me where did all the marks come from. So afraid of being beaten again, I continued to say, "I didn't know, maybe fighting with kids, like I told you earlier." After about thirty minutes or so, I was able to return back to my classroom. Thinking in the back of my mind, that these people are going to get me killed by my father. Afraid of going home and sharing with my mom about what happened at school that day, I decided not to say anything. I stayed in my bedroom for the rest of the evening.

On the following day the Department of Family Services came knocking at my door. Thank goodness I was the one that answered it. The man introduced himself to me, and he asked to speak to my parents. I knew instantly who he was, and what he wanted. I could see that same huge badge on his clothing. Waving my hands towards the man to leave off the porch, while listening to my mother asking me "who's at the door". The man went down the stairs and headed towards his car. I then told my mom that, he had the wrong address. Hoping and praying that he wouldn't return back, but they were determined to locate my parents. They continued to reach out until they got a hold of them.

Later on in life I found out that the case became huge. My parent's Pastor got involved, assisting my parents with the D.C.F.S. case against them. Being interrogated by the state for his abusive behavior, left a question mark in their pastor's mind I'm sure. I was told later on that their pastor spoke on behalf of them, explaining to the state that they were young parents. They were faithful to God's house and they were growing in their faith. After the pastor spoke on their behalf, I wasn't taken out of the home. I remained in my parent's custody. Secretly I wanted to escape to freedom, but the spirit of fear had gripped my heart so tight, and left me paralyzed. The beatings still didn't stop after the encounter with the Department of Family Services.

My childhood was truly a living hell for me. I started to plot and scheme ways in my mind to escape the pain and agony in my life. I felt scared and full of fear most of the time. Thinking there was no sense in living this way anymore. Fear and torment had me hostage. The Spirit of fear grabbed my heart so strongly.

For I know the thoughts that I thinks towards you, said the Lord, thoughts of peace, and not of evil, to give you an expected end.

-Jeremiah 29:11

CHAPTER 4

THE REVOLVING DOOR

My parents believe in helping others, by allowing them to get a head start in life. My parents would allow different family members, or friends of the family to stay with us as long as they needed to. I remember while growing up we lived with five to six different men totally, but not all at once.

It was like a revolving door. One man would leave and another one would come. These men weren't God-fearing men. They were family members from Mississippi who were related to my father. They needed a head start in life and needed somewhere to live until they could care for themselves. So throughout my childhood years, there was always a different male family member living under our roof. Most of the time it was a total of eight people in the house.

Yes, I was unhappy with my father because of the physical and mental abuse. Unfortunately, being physically abused wasn't the end of my story. At the age of twelve, I was also being sexually abused by one of the men who lived with us. This is where the spirit of perversion captured me. One Friday night my parents decided to attend a church service. They left us home with this crazy man who had just moved into our home from out of town. He was my Dad's cousin. This man was crazy indeed. Although I don't like to address someone out of their proper name or character, but for him, I think crazy is dressing him up a bit. For one, he was an alcoholic. He drank all the time. But there was no excuse for what he did to me.

On this particular night, when my parents left for church, I remember my sisters were in their bedrooms, and my brother was in the basement. I was sitting in the living room watching TV. He, the crazy man, was in the living room too. As soon as my parents left out the door, I got up and went to the bathroom. When I went into the bathroom, I had every intention to shut the door behind me as I usually would. Yet to my surprise, he was right behind me and forced his way into the bathroom with me. Locking the door behind him. In the mirror in front of me, I saw him behind me. He grabbed me and put his arm around my neck, telling me to be quiet and don't scream or he would kill my parents. I see myself in the mirror with him pressed up against my body from behind. I can see that I was literally in a state of shock. I was frozen in place. My heart was beating like I'd just run up a flight of stairs. He then moved his hand from around my neck to under my shirt. He fondled my breast. Then still standing behind me, he unzipped my skirt from the front and put his hand down my panties.

There he was, the crazy man, with his filthy hands on me. I can smell the alcohol and must on him. He then turned me around, and put his tongue down my throat. His breath reeked with alcohol. I felt things that I never felt before. I never was touched by anyone before in that way. I knew nothing about sex. The most my mom ever said was to 'keep your dress down'. There I was, still froze. All I got up to do was use the bathroom. Now, needing to go more than ever. He was still threatening me while he was carrying out his pedophile fantasy. I don't know what he could have got out of this. I stood there stiff as a board. He then stopped and left out of the bathroom first. I then finally used the bathroom. I'm surprised I don't urinate on myself. I fixed my clothing back and went to my bedroom that I shared with my two sisters. I got in my bed and cried myself to sleep.

This was my first non-consensual sexual encounter. And it was with a family member. The second encounter, I was fourteen and it occurred with one of my cousins, who I'd grown up with. He would come and spend the night with our family from time to time. At this time, he was about eighteen years old. He was the cousin I confided in. I would talk to him about the physical abuse from my father. We would talk about anything and everything. I felt comfortable being around him and I trusted him with my most intimate thoughts and feelings.

One day he stopped by while my parents were not home. We usually wouldn't let anyone in when my parents weren't at home. However, he was family. I opened the door for him and went back to the kitchen. He followed me into the kitchen. I was sitting there at the kitchen table eating. He took note that my parents were not home. He then came over to me and started to kiss me. Although I did not resist, I knew it was wrong. He then pulled me on over to the kitchen sink and continued to kiss me. He then pulled my skirt up and we had sex there at the sink. I told him to stop, although not wanting him to. Some may say this is consensual sex and not non-consensual, but I did not ask for that. This sexual act left me feeling more violated and filthy inside. Having no self worth. This is where low self-esteem entered into my soul. I had a hard time imaging my first and second sexual encounters were with family members. I knew very little about sex, but I did know that it was wrong, but being physically and mentally abused by father really left me numb and void. Feeling like I was worthless and didn't deserve better, convinced I was born for this. Being someone's punching bag, along with fulfilling lustful and perverted desires for family members. Having sexual intercourse at an early age leaves many major scars in your heart and mind. Take a moment, close your eyes and imagine your daily life being filled with nothing but mental, physical and sexual abuse.

I would ask God, "why am I here?" I didn't quite understand purpose and destiny as a child. All I understood was pain. I believed I was here on earth to endure heartache and pain. Here I am, only a teenager being molested by men that knew better, at the same time physically and mentally and verbally abused by my father. This is where the spirit of hopelessness and depression held me captive.

The very person that should have been your protector and covering wasn't any of those things to me growing up. Instead, he was my abuser. I would ponder, how could I report this sexual abuser to my parents? How can I tell them that the man they allowed into their home was a child molester, and the man you allowed over your children had violated one of them?

I was too afraid to release this information to my parents because I was scared that it would just land me another whopping. I lived with this secret until my adulthood.

But God shows his love for us in that while we were still sinners, Christ died for us. -Roman 5:8

CHAPTER 5

SIXTEEN AND TURNED OUT

Immediately after entering high school I became very promiscuous, sleeping with guys that would give me just a little attention. By the age of fifteen, I was craving for sex. The desire for it grew so strong, perversion and lust was now a part of me. It didn't matter that I had grew up in church, and my home was a God-fearing home. I started skipping classes in ninth grade, running over boys' houses just to have sex. My parents would swing by the school to pick me up at the end of my day. Knowing how strict my father was, I would always return back to the school, before the end of the day for pick up. Trying to hurry back, before the bell sounded off at three thirty, knowing that it was a strong possibility my dad was waiting for me in front of the school. My choices of male friends were not good ones. Most of my boyfriends loved to skip class as well.

I began dating this guy that was so abusive towards me when I wouldn't allow him to have his way with me every time he desired to. He would start slapping me around. Well, I was already adapted to being treated with disrespect, until it really didn't affect me at all anymore. My emotions had died inside of me. I literally couldn't feel anymore. By now I was totally depressed and oppressed, I couldn't focus in school and I was unable to finish homework assignments. My grades were not good in my first year of high school and this led to more whoopings by my father.

Childhood wasn't comfortable for me at all. I was confused and unsure of whom I was in life. Growing up for many years thinking my life had no real value or fruitful meaning. I was strictly called to fulfill lustful desires for nasty and filthy men, or to be someone's punching bag. I felt that I had no real purpose for life!

By my sophomore year of high school, I was totally out there. I had many boyfriends, I started smoking cigarettes. Skipping classes more and more weekly. I remember missing twenty-five days a semester from one class. School was not my focus nor was it my top priority. It was just an escape to meet guys, and enjoy my little six hours of freedom before returning back home.

I was totally not popular with the ladies in high school but I was very popular with the guys. When I did attend classes most of my classmates would spend a large amount of time talking about my shirts and dresses, which really caused me not to focus on the teacher much. I had so much angry and frustration built up inside. I was full of revenge and I was so tired of hearing people's negative words about my dresses. So I would fight, every person that had some negative words concerning my style of dress. I was ready to retaliate for what they'd said about me. I had turned so bitter inside and full of anger. Rage would rise up in me often. I started to feel better inside after getting back at some of my classmates. Fighting them gave me some of my power back. I was bitter and damaged goods, no hope and yearning for my father's heart to love me like a child should be loved.

By this time, I had already experienced more in life than someone forty years old. Lost and confused, totally reckless and dangerous, by the time I turned sixteen I was depressed, oppressed, walking in total rejection and rebellion, and operating in a strong spirit of perversion. I was only seeking for some type of male attention. It really didn't matter who or where it came from. All I knew was I needed it; someone just to tell me I was pretty and that they loved me. After hearing those important words, I believed it would fill the empty void that was deep down in my soul. Those words would bring me comfort and fulfillment. It didn't matter if the boy was cute or ugly; the only think that mattered was he was a male.

By the time I turned seventeen, I was so behind in my classes. One day a light went off in my head after realizing that I was so off track in my studies. I was so unfocused and would not graduate on time if I continued with this dangerous behavior. I was so off course and I needed a new environment.

One morning I left the house as if I was headed for school, but decided to cut class again that day. There was another high school near my home. I decided to stop in simply to see if they would allow me to register without my parents' consent. Knowing that I didn't ask my parents for permission to register in a total different school, I just stepped out to change my current high school on my own. That day I was successful in transferring my classes over to the new school. Thinking by the time I arrived home I was going to get beat down, I walked into the house and explained to my mother that I needed a change of environment. My mother understood and she explained it better to my father when he arrived home. Looking back over that now, it allowed me to graduate on time. Although I was still out there bad and in an unhealthy place emotionally, I was trying hard to refocus and graduate on time.

Determined that I wasn't going to continue with this same behavior in my new school, I started having a desire to graduate, so I could move out and go away to college. I was ready to experience something different from my pass.

By my senior year I began to be more focused on my studies, looking forward to having some freedom, I was finally able to graduate from high school, and I was ready to attend college. My mind began to wonder on ways of escape and graduating from high school and attending college was my way out. Reflecting back on finishing up high school and planning for college, I spoke to my parents about going away to school. I already had a location in mind; it was only six hours away.

Longing and looking forward to having some freedom, graduation was getting closer by the day. Although I was close to graduating I was also totally depressed and very suicidal. All I could think about was finishing school and moving out.

Reflecting back, I recalled sitting my parent

down to discuss with them my desire to go away to college. Yet hearing my father's response literally depressed me more. He said, "I had to attend college here in Chicago, and I had to stay home while going to school. Going away wasn't an option," he stated. "It's unsafe for you to go away to college. The world is dangerous, and people are crazy. You're safe at home attending college." He was adamant. I sat there listening to him and thinking if home is better than I'm in trouble.

Staying home wasn't an option for me at all; I had to think of another way out. Since attending college don't work, now I had to plot another way of escape. All I knew was I was ready to live on my own and I needed to think of another way of accomplishing that.

After graduating from high school, I registered at Columbia College, downtown. This was not the school I had chosen for myself. I felt I was forced into attending. I was not really excited about attending, but I still registered for a few semesters.

With me attending Columbia, I needed a large down payment to hold my classes. Explaining to my father, the five hundred dollars they were requesting would only hold my classes. My father reached into his pack and handed me the money, but before he put the money into my hands, he coached me on what to say to the financial office. I didn't qualify for financial aid at that time and the school was very expensive. My father told me to explain to them that I couldn't afford this amount. He wanted me to tell them I had the deposit but I needed assistance with paying my tuition. After he demonstrated to me how he wanted me to explain the situation, he them told me to repeat in words what he'd just said. I opened my mouth to repeat and before I knew it his fist was in my face. He began screaming and yelling at me, to repeat it just like he said it. I was standing by the bathroom where he was, crying and bawling my eyes out. Face red as fire, jaws stuck to my teeth. Looking for blood to fall out of my mouth the pain was so bad. My face started pounding with severe pain and discomfort.

He said to me again, repeat it just like I told you to say it. I was standing there, head hurting so bad from just getting slipped in my face. Thinking, I just graduated from high school, getting ready to attend college still getting slapped in my face with my dad's fist.

I'm ready to escape this prison, by now I'm totally suicidal. I did not want to live like this anymore. I wanted out of that house, freedom truly came with a high price for me. By this time I lost my desire to attend college, I just wanted to move out. Getting out on my own was in the front of my thoughts daily. Eighteen years old, still getting beat by my father's fist, realizing I had made some unhealthy decisions, but that particular day was the last straw for me. Fed up with all of it! I'm getting out of this house, no matter what!

I started dating this handsome guy that lived down the street from me. We attended high school together for a few years, and after I graduated we began dating. We fell in love after dating for a year in a half and decided to get married. My freedom had finally come, at least I thought so.

He healeth the broken in heart, and bind up their wounds. -Psalms 147:3

Chapter 6

Wounded and Broken

Married and broken, pregnant with my first child and wounded. I had started a new life unprepared and untrained for adulthood. I desired freedom but was still trapped in my mind and body. Trusting men was not a place I could let my hair down and relax. I had a difficult time believing anything a man had to say. Even though I fell in love and had gotten married didn't mean I was complete and whole. Distrust was a major issue I'd dealt with all my life. Therefore, I carried that same behavior into my marriage. Marriage and distrust cannot operate on the same page.

When you're forced to grow up in the fast line, you end up missing a lot in the process. I was forced to rush through my childhood, determined to escape my pain and agony. Challenged daily in my mind if I wanted to even stay on this earth. Miserable and full of heartache and so much inner pain.

For years I dealt with un-forgiveness, and all the hurt and pain that had increased inside. It was so built up inside of me, I would take it out on everyone else, yelling and screaming all the time. My soul wasn't at peace. Daily, I was feeling nothing but heartache and pain. Relationships and friendships were difficult to maintain and keep. There was an empty void, and a deep wound inside of me, I was damaged goods and scarred for life.

I grew up looking for love in all the wrong places. Searching for acceptance and validation from a man. Seeking attention from anyone who would offer it to me. Looking for a love and comparison from people that really didn't have it to offer. The type of love I was looking and seeking for, I felt didn't really exist.

For God so love the world that her give his only begotten son, that whosoever believed in him shall not perish but have everlasting life. -John 3:16

CHAPTER 7

GOD REACHED FOR ME

Even though I was raised in a holiness church all my life, I really didn't know God on a personal level. Church was just routine and mandatory by my parents. A relationship with God didn't exist and I didn't quite understand who God was and what he wanted with me. After I was married I decided to stop attending Church, I really didn't have a desire. I didn't quite understand the purpose for it, frankly it was just too time consuming for me. Usually when you're forced to do something, once you're all grown up you lose interest, so church wasn't my life nor was God a part of it, I didn't return back for many years.

Carrying on with my life, by this time I was married with two children Louis and Kevin. I began having a strong desire to become a nurse, as I was approaching twenty-eight years old. I returned back to college still ignorant of true purpose in fulfilling God's plans for my life. All I knew was I had a strong desire to help people, especially women who had walked in the same shoes I'd walked in. I was unsure as to where this new desire had come from and I had many mixed emotions. I was still bitter and angry all the time. I would take it out mostly on my husband and children. The pain was still so strong inside from my childhood.

In 1998, I started attending College for Nursing. I had already worked as a certified nursing assistant for ten years. I began nursing school because I couldn't shake this strong desire inside of me for more.

Attending classes, minding my own business, God began to reach for me doing classroom time and in clinical sites. I didn't understand what was going on inside of me. I know I needed a God ordain moment, because I didn't understand God's plan for my life at all.

I recall God connecting me with a young lady. She had every class and every clinical site I had.

She would follow me around doing clinical training. It was as if she were drawn to me like a magnet. Every time I sat down she would sit next to me or around me. Every time she opened her mouth, she was telling me sometime about Jesus and how good He was. She would tell me how He died for my sins on the cross. As she ministered to me tears would flow from my eyes, I would literally be almost wailing in class, about to break down. I would change my seat often but this girl wouldn't stop! I pondered, "who is this lady, and who sent her to me"?

She was so focused on her assignment that she wouldn't stop; determined to succeed at her God given assignment. I told her I already knew God, that I was raised up in the Church all my life. That didn't get her off my back, she then looked at me, and said, "yes, you might have been raised up in Church, but God is looking for you in this season to serve him." Tears began flowing from my eyes, I was speechless!.

This lady was so aggressive and determined in

her assignment, she was reaching my heart through the word of God. I said to her, "Shaletha Malden if you stop making me cry in class, I'll go to church with you one Sunday morning." I decided to visit her church like I promised her and I had an awesome experience in God that day. God literally visited me in the service. On my first visit back to God's house he changed my life. The power of God was so strong on me that day. The next Sunday determined to attend again, my classmate wasn't there. I didn't know she had to work that Sunday morning. I decided to stay anyway and truly enjoyed the service again. God touched me so that Sunday I joined the following Sunday, and have remained in church ever since. This young lady ministered to me eighteen years ago and we're best friends still today. God had a divine plan for my life.

Behold the Lord's hand is not to shortened, that he cannot save. Neither his ears to heavy that he cannot hear. -Isaiah 59:1

CHAPTER 8

PURPOSE BEGINS TO TAKE FORM

I can't believe that God had a plan for somebody like me; someone, who was totally messed up inside. How could God use someone that was full of so many broken pieces? Thinking in the back of my mind that God truly has His work cut out for Him in dealing with me. I was so damaged. God's hand began to move within my spirit as the preached word of God began to dig up some hidden areas in my soul, things begin to come into surface.

Change had just begun to invade my life. Crying every Sunday morning when the word of God was being preached. Attending my classmate's church faithfully, I decided to joined as a member, under the leadership of Bishop Alvin Evans, Love Center Greater Works C.O.G.I.C, on the west side of Chicago, IL. I remained under his leadership for five years, receiving salvation there. I grew by leaps and bound, God's word was touching my heart every Sunday morning. My pastor and his wife put me in the position as his personal nurse. I begin working in the church faithful. Traveling with my pastor as he would go out to different places to minister the gospel. I was serving as his nurse faithfully, enjoying operating in this area of ministry. God would use the Man of God and his wife to speak into my life. Even though I was in church now, I was still dealing with a lot of childhood issues, and from time to time my issues would surface. I needed a lot of help, healing and much deliverance. By 2002, I had walked into the office of an Evangelist, pressing and moving forward in the things of God. I remember desiring and wanting more of God. I didn't recognize back then, that true growth and development in the things of God comes from being on your knees first.

In 2004, I joined under the leadership of Apostle Johnston L. Swain, God's True Love Ministries, Chicago, IL. This was the beginning of my deliverance process; demons were being cast out of me almost weekly. I was operating in ministry assuming that I was good. I had already stepped out and was operating in the things of God, not really understanding to the fullness, that I needed to be totally healed and delivered from all of my inward garbage that had built-up inside. I began to see God in a totally different light; He placed me under this Man of God for deliverance. I didn't understand what was happening inside of me. One day my girlfriend sat me down and began to explain to me that I must be delivered from my childhood before God could use me effectively.

In 2004, God set me up! This was heaven's ordained time, and season to begin to pull out the spirit of rejection, hatred, un-forgiveness, low-self-esteem, lust, perversion, depression, rebellion, and fear.

CHAPTER 9

BEING PURGED FOR PURPOSE

Deep down inside of me was the spirit of unforgiveness. Yes, the hand of God had reached down for me. Yes, his hand was on me strong, but I still needed a lot of deliverance. I was back in church faithfully, going every Sunday morning. Yet haven't dealt with the strong man of unforgiveness. I had held on to so much hurt and anger all of my life. Sitting down in church mad and upset at my father. I had grown into the place where I would love to praise and worship God every Sunday morning but then throughout the week, I couldn't stand to look my father in his face. Full of hatred and frustration; evil thoughts had taken over my mind and emotions. I just wanted him totally out of my life. Mixed feelings daily, recalling many days as well as holidays I was unable to sit down in his presence too long. After about twenty minutes or so, my voice had escalated into yelling and screaming at him for something.

By this time my children were ten and seven years old. They would always ask to visit their grandparents. After taking them over to visit, after a while I would catch myself ready to fight my daddy. By now un-forgiveness had totally manifested in me and I still hadn't dealt with the spirit of revenge and anger. Churching on Sunday morning, ready to fight my father by Monday night.

I didn't really know how to get beyond all the heartache from my past. I didn't really know how to let go and release it all to God. I can recall one holiday sitting at my parent's house on Linder street. My father said something to me and I exploded. It usually didn't take much to set me off. By now I was yelling at the top of my lungs. My oldest son Louis looked up to me and said, "why are you so mad at granddaddy mom". I went straight into denial. I said, "I'm fine. I'm not mad at your grandfather." Louis looked at me; at this time, he was only ten years old. He said, "yes mom you're angry at granddad for something". I was so amazed at my child, speaking reality to my spirit man. That day a light sat off inside of me, my son was right, I was angry and bitter, I needed to be delivered from this stronghold of un-forgiveness.

By this time, I was fully inside of church, worshiping and praising God every Sunday morning. I could recall sitting in church under a powerful move of God and was manifesting out demons almost every other service. Pastor was laboring with me just about week after week. And I can recall many services, either running from him, or trying to sit down in a corner somewhere. Through many anointed services, God, by his Spirit would increase Pastor's spiritual vision to see the mess inside of me, and here we go again, he was casting out spirits and calling them out by name almost week after week for two years straight.

By 2008, I began to see some freedom. Un-forgiveness, hatred, lust and perversion, bitterness, fear, depression and suicidal thoughts were totally out of my soul.

Yet the spirit of low self-esteem, and no self-worth hang out for many years after. I was delivered from many other different things. I had a hard time freeing my soul from my father's words he had spoken over me as a child. "You will never become nothing in life. You will never have nothing". Those words had so much power over me; I spent years and years trying to prove my father wrong. I would become successful. I would accomplish everything I put my hands to touch. I wouldn't be left behind. It was as if I was in forward movement daily. Pushing myself to become better and do better. A deep spirit of doubt and unbelief had deeply taken root inside of me. Wanting so much to be the best I could be, sometimes finding myself moving and running pass God. I really could never believe people when they would say to me, you're successful, you're going to succeed at many things. Those words would just fly over my head. I was not looking for approval from people; I was looking for approval from my father.

I was so determined to make my father eat those words. I'm striving daily to be successful in life. This behavior put me into speed mode. Just another area I needed some deliverance in.

CHAPTER 10

FREEDOM IN FORGIVENESS

In 2009, my relationship with my father was much better. I'd stopped crying myself to sleep every night. We were communicating much better. My father had been in ministry about seven years at this point; God had called him to preach and pastor. God's hand was on his life as well, working on the inside of him. Even though God was dealing with him, I couldn't join his ministry. I attempted twice, but I couldn't receive from his table at all. Yes, I believed my father was called by God for a work as well, but I had been destroyed by him so that I couldn't totally allow him to minister to me spiritually.

There needed to be some natural healing and building up, some coming together and bonding first. How can two walk together unless they agree? Agreement was being worked on in the spirit realm. Rebuilding and reestablishing our relationship took time, many years and many conversations. Trust had to be reestablished and fear had to resolve.

A few years after God had called him into ministry, my father apologized for all the beatings and whooping I had to endure for many years. He explained to me that this behavior came from his father as well, and that was all he knew at the time. Those words begin to touch my heart, and tears begin to flow from my eyes. Yes, God had already healed me, but just hearing those words come out of my father's mouth touched my heart and soul. God was breaking all of us down to our knees. Finally, the father I strongly desired and spent years longing and looking for the daddy I was missing out of my life, was finally here. Well, by this time I was grown. Married with two children. Even though many years had passed, these powerful words were the missing link. Those words were healing for my soul; finally I could get my power back. After searching for many years for a strong father figure for my life, God had cleaned and restored our father-daughter relationship.

CHAPTER 11

HEALED AND WHOLE

Major changes have taken place in my heart and soul. I'd never imagined God changing my life like He did. He impacted my life with so many awesome and powerful people in the faith to help guide me along; pushing and motivating me to press into purpose.

Now I'm finally healed from my childhood trauma and tragedies. Life appears so much clearer now. Even though I lost so much in the fire, God replaced it with greater. Freedom is finally here, and I'm starting to relax and enjoy every moment of it.

Yes, the process was rough and very difficult; God by his faithful hand guided my foot steps, He held my hand through each bumpy road, and every dark dead end street. Yes, blinded by my dark path, God yet found me and placed me on His path of freedom and healing. Then God placed a deep desire and hunger inside of me to help many women enduring the same journey I had to endure; encouraging them that they can make it out, through the help of God. Drawing closer to God has changed my life greatly. I realized and understood that it was nobody but God's grace and mercy that kept me. By God's power and authority, He didn't allow the devil to take me out. All praises and glory belongs to the almighty God that sits high above the earth. While He's sitting high, he's looking low in the earth realm watching over His creation and His children. So I bless God for it all. This is my life story. Was my live journey a tragedy or destiny? It was truly a challenging walk towards destiny.

The transformation of the power of God will come to lift you out of that lonely place. It doesn't matter where you've been. His hand still reaches for you, even in that dark place. You're still called and anointed by the almighty God for an assigned work in the earth realm. He didn't change his mind about you, just because you detoured for a while. His hand is still on your life. And his love for you grows stronger each day. It's God's will that you be free from all hurt and pain. Your journey was assigned to help someone else; you're able now to speak into the life of many women because of your pass. Through your testimony God will heal many women from that place of brokenness and being bound by the enemy. Hold your head up ladies, you're still God's mouthpiece in the earth realm. His promises still rest on your head. Be encouraged and continue to allow the transformation of the power of God to continue to touch your life. Rest and walk in the power of God.

And we know that all things work together for the good to them that love God, to them who are the called according to his purpose.
– Romans 8:28

ENCOURAGEMENT TO YOUNG WOMEN

Women know that you're truly special in the eyesight of God, called and chosen by Him for a work. God loves you and you're the apple of His eye. It doesn't matter where you've been or what you've done in your life, you're still called by God for a purpose and an assignment work. You're unique and worth great value in God's vision. He designed and made you just like he wanted you to be. Just because you had some major challenges that has hit your life doesn't cost you out of the equation.

Great trials and tribulations in life just means you have a great work to complete for God in the earth. Love yourself and know that you're beautiful to the Lord. You can make it with the help of God. He's strengthened you for the walk with him, and you shall walk in great integrity and destiny knowing that your pass life won't stop your future, or hinder your destiny. It's all working and coming together for the glory of God. Change has hit your life for the better, and you shall be all that God has called and equipped you to be in Jesus name.

ABOUT THE AUTHOR

Born on a cold brisk winter day in Tchula, Mississippi, Alisa is the daughter of Dave and Fannie Howard. At the age of four her entire family transitioned to Chicago, IL. She attended George Collins High School and attended and graduated from Triton College, receiving a certification as a Licensed Practical Nurse.

In 2011 she received a Bachelors of Theology and in 2013 she received her Masters of Divinity under Grace Seminary School of Ministry in South Carolina, under the leadership of Dr. Dean Lilly English.. Alisa is the proud mother of two children, Louis and Kevin and the proud grandmother of Nathan.

Alisa was raised in Church but received Christ in her life in 1999. She is a member of God's True Love Ministries under the leadership of Apostle Jonathan L. Swain of Chicago, IL., currently serving on the intercessory prayer team, and currently teaching Sunday School. Alisa also hosts prayer gatherings through her personal outreach ministry, Preparing The Way of the Lord Ministries

Alisa's desire is to reach as many women in this world through my testimony.

Made in the USA
Charleston, SC
13 April 2016